MARTHA BLACK

GOLD RUSH PIONEER

20/82

Martha Black

GOLD RUSH PIONEER

CAROL MARTIN

DOUGLAS & McINTYRE
VANCOUVER / TORONTO / BUFFALO

The excerpt on page 38 is reprinted from *Klondike: The Last Great
Gold Rush, 1896–1899*, by Pierre Berton. Used by permission.

Douglas & McIntyre
585 Bloor Street West
Toronto, Ontario M6G 1K5

Distributed in the U.S. by Publishers Group West
4065 Hollis Street
Emeryville, CA 94608

Canadian Cataloguing in Publication Data
Martin, Carol
Martha Black : gold rush pioneer
ISBN 1-55054-245-1

1. Black, Martha Louise, 1866–1957. 2. Women Pioneers -
Yukon Territory - Biography. 3. Klondike River Valley
(Yukon) - Gold discoveries.* I. Title.
FC4022.1.B54M3 1996   971.9'102'092   C96-930043-3
F1091.M3 1996

Maps and cover lettering and illustration by Jack McMaster
Design by Michael Solomon
Printed and bound in Canada

The publisher gratefully acknowledges the assistance of the Canada
Council and of the British Columbia Ministry of Tourism, Small
Business and Culture.

CONTENTS

To my daughter, Pamela

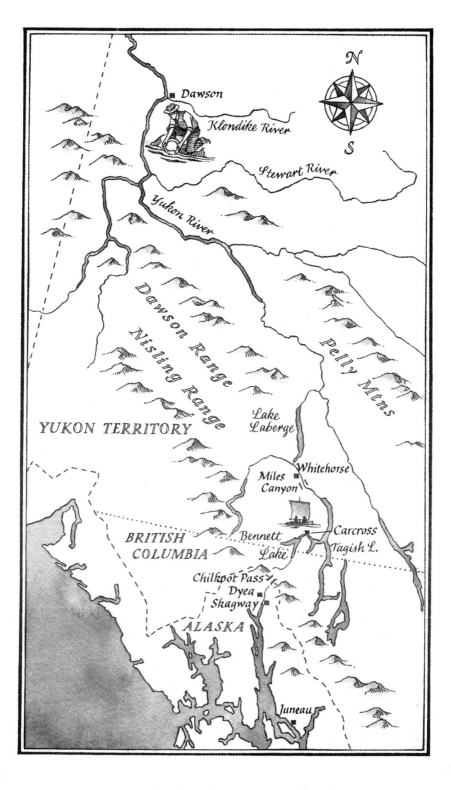

1

FIRE, FIRE, EVERYWHERE!

"HURRY! Hurry!" cried Martha's father as he dashed into the house. His face was black with smoke. "The whole town's afire. We must run for our lives!"

Martha Munger was only five years old, but she was frightened. All through the house, the adults rushed around in panic and confusion.

Martha's mother and the servants quickly gathered a few blankets and warm clothes. Soon everyone was running from the house, taking only what they could carry. For Martha that meant her favourite rag doll, Louisa, and her grandmother's treasured silver spoons.

It was a cold October night in 1871 when the famous Chicago fire swept through the city. The countryside had been suffering from a severe drought. Then, so the story goes, Mrs. O'Leary's cow kicked over a lamp in her stable—one of the many in Chicago.

The firemen were already worn out from struggling with fires all summer, but the blaze that started that evening was different. The flames soon engulfed the city. The fire raged for days. Before it was over, more

THE GREAT FIRE AT CHICAGO, OCT. 8TH 1871.

Before photography was common, the firm of Currier & Ives created prints to record special scenes or events. These prints were drawn by artists, reproduced by lithography and coloured by hand. The prints were cheap and could be found everywhere.

In the nineteenth century, buildings were mostly made of wood, and fire could easily destroy a city. Pictures of fires were particularly popular, and the Chicago fire was one of the most famous.

---

than 100,000 people had been burned out of their homes. Three hundred people were dead, and the city was a shambles.

Lost to the flames was the Mungers' beautiful big house with its elegant bay windows. Also gone was the new building that held Martha's father's laundry business.

Soon the family was loaded onto a horse-drawn wagon. There was Martha, her mother, her baby sister Agnes and Aunt Edith, who had been sick in bed for weeks and had to be helped into the wagon. The servants hurried after them on foot.

Martha was frightened, but she was excited, too. She loved an adventure.

The streets were crowded with people trying to escape the approaching flames. Martha's eyes were stinging, and her throat burned from the thick black smoke that filled the air. Frightened adults, crying children and terrified horses and cattle all scrambled in one direction. Chicago was built on the shore of Lake Michigan. If they could reach the water, they would be safe.

Finally Martha and her family arrived at the lake. Here the wind was cold and, like many others, they huddled around a small cooking fire on the beach. Soon soldiers arrived to stand guard in case looters tried to take advantage of the homeless families. As evening fell, the Mungers wrapped themselves in the blankets they had brought from home. They curled up under the wagon and went to sleep.

For three days the Mungers lived on the shore of Lake Michigan along with thousands of others. Martha played by the water. She helped to cook potatoes in the coals of the fires that were kept burning night and day. For her it was like a summer holiday at the beach. But for most of the citizens of Chicago, it would be remembered as the most horrifying experience of their lives.

2

LEARNING TO BE A LADY

THE Chicago fire destroyed the Mungers' laundry business. Their house was burned to the ground. For a man who had provided well for his family, it was humiliating to have to start over. George Munger had been a poor young man when he married Martha's mother, but he had worked hard to make a success of his business. Now he would have to begin again.

The family and their servants were squeezed into four rooms in one of the small houses that had been hastily built for the victims of the fire. Martha called it a shack, and the neighbourhood soon became known as Poverty Flats.

It was a difficult time for the Mungers as they struggled to get back on their feet. They were saddened, too, by the loss of Aunt Edith, who had died during the ordeal on the beach. "She won't have any more pain," Martha's mother said when she told Martha what had happened.

Poverty Flats was close to a part of town that had not been burned down. One day Martha was playing with some of the children who had not lost anything in the fire. One of their mothers saw her wearing her cheap gingham dress (not at all like the beautiful clothes that she had once owned). The woman called Martha a "rag-tag-bobtail" child and sent her home. Martha vowed then never to judge others by their appearance.

But the unhappy days didn't last long. The Mungers were lucky. They had a close-knit family who helped them through this difficult time. Soon Martha's father had the laundry business back in operation.

The family wash was one of the great unsolved housekeeping problems of those times. Washing was done at home on a scrub board or in a hand-cranked washer and wringer. It was exhausting work. Laundry businesses with their steam power were very popular for those who could afford it. So George Munger's business flourished. Before long he had outlets operating throughout the country, and the Mungers were able to move into a new brick house near Lincoln Park, an area of large homes, hotels and trees.

Chicago had been a booming city even before the fire. Its location on the Great Lakes made it a major port and, with the growth of the railways, it became a shipping centre for the whole country. Before the fire, all the buildings had been made of wood. Afterwards, the houses, factories and offices were replaced with structures of stone and steel. Chicago became one of the most innovative and modern cities on the continent—and the second biggest city in the United States.

The fire wasn't the only tragedy the Mungers had faced. Within four years of her marriage, Martha's mother had had five children. The death of a newborn was quite common at that time, before the discovery of antibiotics and other modern medicines. Three Munger children had died at birth or as infants. Martha's sister Agnes probably had infantile paralysis. She was never able to walk and died before she was two.

When Martha was six years old, her brother George was born. After this, her mother was sick for a long time, and Martha was sent to live with her grandparents. They were loving but strict. Like other little girls in well-to-do families, she learned to sew samplers. She embroidered sayings such as "God Bless Our Home," and the texts were then framed and hung on the wall. Every day while she worked at her samplers, her grandfather would read from one of his favourite novels, perhaps something by Charles Dickens or Sir Walter Scott.

As a child, Martha was particularly fascinated by the stories of the independent women in her family. There was her great-great-great-grandmother Stebbins, who saved the family from an Indian attack, and her great-aunt Sophronia, who had been condemned to burn at the stake as a witch, but was saved through her kindness to the jailer's family.

Martha was proud of the men in the family, too. The first Munger had arrived in Connecticut in 1645 and, over the years, members of the family had fought in the American Revolution, the War of 1812 and the American Civil War.

Martha was a good student, but she was quick-tempered and always getting into trouble. She wanted to try everything! Once she surprised her mother by arriving home in a hearse—the driver couldn't resist her polite request. Her most famous escapade was escaping from her grandparents at the circus and going up in a hot-air balloon, a treat that had been strictly forbidden.

When she was thirteen, Martha started high school. Two years later she was sent to what was known as a finishing school. At Lake Forest Select Seminary for Young Ladies, she was supposed to learn all the social graces required of a young woman. But she often neglected to follow the rules. After one too many complaints from her teachers, Martha's parents decided to look for a stricter school. Her mother had been educated in a convent. Perhaps this would be the answer for Martha.

Somewhat surprisingly, Martha spent five very happy years at St. Mary's of Notre Dame in Indiana. The girls at the school were very protected, from the time they were picked up at the train station until they were delivered safely back at the end of the term. They were allowed to write two letters home each week, but only under the strict supervision of the Sisters. They learned to curtsey perfectly to a large picture of Queen Victoria.

Martha's parents wanted to prepare her to be a good wife and mother, the normal future for a young woman at that time. But while she enjoyed her years at St. Mary's, Martha felt that it did little to prepare her for such a role. She did learn the social graces that were so important for young women in society. As she described it, "I danced, played and sang a little, recited 'with so much expression,' did fine needlework, painted china and watercolour pictures." She learned how to make lemon cream pie and angel cake and was told how "to dress for and act at receptions, dinner-parties, musicales and dances."

The school taught academic subjects as well. Some of these proved to be of more importance to Martha in her future life than she imagined at the time. One of her favourite subjects was botany. She had always had a special fondness for flowers, and St. Mary's prided itself on its beautiful gardens. On graduation, Martha won an award for her herbarium, a collection of dried and mounted plants. She also learned to type, a skill that was just coming into fashion. But the elocution lessons—practice in giving formal recitations of poems—were what she enjoyed most. They helped her develop her natural ability to speak before an audience, a talent that later served her well.

Martha was head of her class. Her only disappointment on graduation day was that while the heads of the other classes wore blameless gold or silver wreaths, she worn green, a sign that in terms of conduct she had just "got by."

3

ALL GROWN UP

WHEN Martha returned from school, she had become, as she later wrote, a young lady whose chief mission in life was to wait until the "right" man came along to marry her. She was now allowed to go to evening parties at the homes of friends, but her protective father always took her and picked her up. At one party she met Will Purdy, the son of the president of the Chicago, Rock Island and Pacific Railway. Martha and Will became good friends.

George Munger now had more than seventy laundries across the country. He was a successful and wealthy member of Chicago society. He took Martha to lectures and introduced her to many of the interesting speakers who came through Chicago. At a time when there was no television, no radio and no movies, attending lectures was a popular way to spend an evening.

Martha's parents had had another baby while she was away at school, a little girl they named Belle. Her mother was again very slow in recovering from the birth and had become an invalid. Her father was planning to retire and move the family to the country. Martha accompanied him on a trip to buy a ranch in Kansas. While passing through Denver, they visited her Aunt Ione.

Aunt Ione was an unusually independent woman for her time, and she took an active interest in politics. She later became the first woman to be elected to the Denver school board.

At her aunt's home, Martha met a number of women involved in the suffrage movement, which was dedicated to winning for women the right to vote. Among them was one of their most famous leaders, Susan B. Anthony. The ideas these women discussed appealed to the independent-minded Martha.

Back home in Chicago, Martha enjoyed the parties, the dancing and the beautiful clothes that were part of Chicago's high society, but she didn't like the restrictions young women faced at that time. (Once her father, who considered "paint and powder" immoral for a young girl like Martha, threw out her treasured box of French makeup, saying, "Your mother never used this stuff.")

Will Purdy was usually at the parties and outings. Martha seemed to see him everywhere. Soon they were in love.

Will was a very eligible young man. He was from a good family and had a job with the Rock Island Railway with a salary of a thousand dollars a year. Before long the two were planning a wedding, with the approval of both their families. Martha was twenty-one years old.

In her usual enthusiastic way, Martha threw herself into the activities expected of a young woman about to be a bride. She embroidered cushions and scarves for the furniture. She made needlepoint covers for chairs.

She painted china. She decorated pieces of furniture with the then popular burnt designs made with a heated poker. And for the first time, Martha's love of clothes was completely satisfied when dressmakers were hired to make beautiful gowns and matching hats for her trousseau.

Martha's mother was not well enough to be part of an elaborate ceremony, so the wedding itself was a simple one. But the newlywed couple began life with everything they could possibly want. Martha's father gave them a house not far from Chicago, in Walden. The wedding gifts that flooded in took care of most of the furnishings. They had a maid to do the routine household work, so Martha had plenty of time to herself. She wrote poems, and some were even published in the Chicago papers. And she worked on her collection of pressed and mounted wildflowers, studying their formation and experimenting with ways to retain their shapes and colours.

One of the major benefits of marriage for Martha was that she was now free to go out unchaperoned. Young women in wealthy families were closely protected until they were married. They spent most of their days at home with their mothers, or they were accompanied everywhere, usually by a family member. After she was married, even a simple trip to a shop with other young wives seemed exciting.

In many ways Martha's open and adventurous character was formed by the times and the place in which she lived. The late nineteenth century was a period of exuberant invention that led to the development of all kinds of automated machinery. There were streetlights and

People went crazy over bicycles during the 1890s. Almost everyone had one. There was even a bicycle for ten called the decemtuple. Martha and Will were the proud owners of a tandem, a bicycle built for two.

Bicycling led to a new style of clothing for women. The Gibson girl look was named for the artist Charles Dana Gibson, whose drawings were published in *Life*, the new weekly magazine. Gibson drew tall, wholesome-looking women wearing shirt-like blouses and straight skirts. This outfit was very different from the clothing traditionally worn by most women of style, whose elaborate corsets, bustles and full skirts let others know that they did not need to do any manual work.

Along with the new clothes, a new freedom was just beginning for women—freedom to take an active part in life, in sports and, for some, even in work. Martha's bicycling costume included velveteen bloomers, named for Amelia Bloomer, a women's rights reformer.

streetcars in the cities. There were typewriters in the offices, and telegraph companies were able to send messages swiftly across the continent for the first time. Soon everyone was beginning to use the new Kodak camera. Alexander Graham Bell had perfected the telephone in 1875, and its use spread quickly throughout North America.

It was a boom period for railways, too. In Canada, the Canadian Pacific Railway reached the west coast in 1885, two years before Martha and Will were married. By the 1890s, five rail lines spanned the United States.

4

THE GAY NINETIES

WITHIN a year, Martha and Will's first child, Warren, was born. Martha loved being a mother and running a home. She looked forward to having a large family. When Warren was old enough to go to kindergarten—one of the first in the city—she took him there every day and stayed to help teach the children games and crafts. With her housework well-organized and a maid to help, Martha had plenty of free time.

Before long, however, her second son, Donald, arrived. Busy with a new baby, she gave up her work at the kindergarten. While the boys were young, her life revolved around them. Meanwhile, Will was busy with increased responsibilities at the railway and was away from home for days at a time. They started to drift apart.

When both boys were old enough to go to school, daily life changed for Martha. The early years of what were known as the Gay Nineties were full of fun and entertainment for the wealthy. They attended lectures. They went to musical comedies and Shakespearean theatre. Martha and the other wives in her circle attended

The Chicago World's Fair in 1893 was a coming of age for the city. About 27 million people from around the world paid fifty cents to see the fair's stunning electrical and mechanical displays, and to line up for a ride on the world's first Ferris wheel. The buildings created for the fair influenced the future of American architecture and made Chicago an important cultural centre. As a member of the city's social élite, Martha was involved in many of the activities and parties. This poster not only commemorated the 400th anniversary of Columbus's voyage, but was a memorial to the famous Chicago fire, still a vivid memory for Martha.

luncheons and played euchre, or they went to the Turkish baths. On the last Thursday of every month, Martha was "at home," which meant this was when friends were expected to call. She served them hot chocolate with whipped cream, sandwiches and cake.

All these entertainments were hardly enough for a woman as full of curiosity and energy as Martha. But it was impossible for her to take a job. Women at her level of society just didn't do that. Instead they became involved in social work. European immigrants were flooding into the country at a fantastic rate. For many, life in the slums of the city was one of poverty and hunger.

A number of women began donating their time to relieve this suffering, especially for the children. One of the most famous was Jane Addams. She created what became known as settlement houses. With classes, gyms and nursery schools for the poor, settlement houses were places where society women could find useful work when the ordinary work world remained closed to them. Martha threw her energies into collecting money to buy food, clothing and coal for the poor.

Wealthy women also joined clubs—often organizations with a mission. For Martha this was the Women's Auxiliary to the Cuban Committee of One Hundred in support of the Cuban rebellion of 1895. She wrote letters, raised money and made speeches on behalf of the Cuban people. It became a popular cause in the United States and led to the Spanish-American War of 1898. Years later Martha recognized that she had had little understanding of the Cuban situation and felt strongly about the need to promote peace rather than war.

Martha enjoyed what Chicago had to offer, and she involved herself in the issues of the day. But by the time she had been married for ten years, she was bored. "I was thoroughly disillusioned with youth's ideal of life," she wrote, "and miserably unhappy." When a fortune-teller looked at her palm in 1897 and told her that she would leave the country within a year and face dangers, hardship and sorrow, it sounded like a wild fantasy.

5

GOLD!

"**S**ACKS of Gold from Mines of the Clondyke" screamed a headline in the San Francisco *Chronicle* on July 15, 1897.

Just when Martha was bored with her life and longing for adventure, the whole of North America was swept up in excitement. Gold had been discovered in the Canadian North.

There had been tales of gold in the Klondike River Valley for decades. The river flows across the middle of what is now the Yukon Territory. It joins up with the Yukon River before entering Alaska and moving on towards the Bering Strait.

For hundreds of centuries, these ancient rivers had carved valleys through the mountains. Their grinding force had uncovered gold, in nuggets, grains and dust. The gold was carried along by the water until its weight drew it to the bottom of the river bed. Here it lay in a pure, available form—placer gold.

But this distant and rugged land had only a small, mostly Native population. During its long dark winters, the sun barely lightened the horizon, and the temperature could drop to fifty degrees below freezing. The interior could be reached only by river or over dangerous mountain passes. It was a journey that outsiders had seldom been willing or able to make. Those who did were mostly loners seeking the freedom to live as they wished, accountable to no one.

All of this changed after August 16, 1896. That was when George Carmack, Skookum Jim and Dawson Charlie made a discovery that would change life in the Yukon forever. In Rabbit Creek, just above the spot where it enters the Klondike River, they uncovered a thumb-sized nugget of gold. Before the day was over, they had panned the creek for a rich harvest. They then passed on the news of the discovery to others in the territory. (It was part of the prospectors' code to share information about a new find with anyone else working the same area.)

Soon everyone was placing claims on what had become known as Bonanza Creek. But the true size of the find didn't reach the outside world until July of the following year, when the miners, carrying bags filled with gold, poured off the steamship *Excelsior* in San Francisco. Two days later a second ship, the *Portland*, steamed into Seattle carrying two tons of gold.

The stampede was on. Soon Seattle was overflowing with young and old, rich and poor, all determined to make their fortune in the Klondike. Within two weeks, nine ships, packed with would-be miners, were ready to sail north.

Back in Chicago, everyone was talking about the possibility of making a fortune in the Klondike. Martha and Will were as excited as everyone else. Before long they were beginning to make plans to take part in the great adventure.

Will Purdy and his friend Eli Gage were eager to join the rush to the Canadian North and become what were soon known as stampeders or argonauts. Their fathers, both wealthy businessmen, were enthusiastic about the idea of having a stake in the gold, and they agreed to finance the venture. The whole thing was to be done in style. They formed their own company and bought their own boats so they could be sure of good transportation.

Martha and Eli's wife, Sophy, were longing to go, too. It was a story by William Lambert, one of the men who worked for Will's father, that provided the excuse for Martha to join the expedition. Lambert showed them a copy of a will written by a relative of his who had died in the Klondike. In it a million dollars in gold, as well as some valuable property, was left to the Lambert family. He was looking for someone to go up and claim the inheritance for them. Whoever went could keep half of the gold.

It seems strange that a society woman like Martha would make plans to head for the remote and wild Yukon. But a kind of madness had seized the world, especially the United States, when the gold was discovered. The most unlikely people, knowing little about the country they were heading for or the problems they would encounter along the way, made plans to join the stampede.

Martha told herself that it was a wonderful chance to provide luxuries for herself and her children. But it was more likely the idea of taking part in an adventure that persuaded her to leave her children for a wild goose

True to form, Martha outfitted herself in style for her adventure. Her wardrobe included woollen stockings and underwear (called "combinations," or long johns) and high leather boots. The highlight was what was called an outing costume—the latest thing for women doing something even mildly strenuous. Martha described it as "made of heavily ribbed tobacco-brown corduroy velvet with a skirt of shockingly immodest length (it actually showed my ankles), five yards around the

bottom, edged with brush braid, and lined with brown silk and interlined with a foot of buckram, which gave it a fetching swing as I walked. It had a Norfolk jacket with many pleats, a blouse with a high stiff collar almost to my ears and a pair of voluminous brown silk bloomers, which came below the knee."

Martha had no idea just how dangerous and strenuous an "outing" she was about to undertake!

chase. What is more surprising is that her family encouraged her. Her parents agreed to take care of Warren and Donald at their ranch in Kansas. The boys were still young—Warren ten and Donald six—but it was only to be for the summer, and they would enjoy a holiday with their grandparents.

Martha took the boys to Kansas before heading north. When she arrived, she discovered that her brother, George, and a cousin, Harry Peachey, had caught gold rush fever, too. Martha encouraged them to join her and Will.

They met Will in Denver and soon all four were on their way to Seattle. From there they were to take one of the company boats to Skagway in Alaska. From Skagway they would travel inland to Dawson, where they would meet up with Eli and Sophy, who planned to sail north from San Francisco.

But things did not go as planned.

While waiting for the boat in Seattle, Will received a telegram from Eli calling him to San Francisco on business. From there he wrote back to Martha to say that he had heard terrible stories about the trip to Dawson. He was thinking instead of going to Hawaii, then known as the Sandwich Islands. The islands had recently been annexed by the United States, and Will thought that there would be good opportunities for him there. He suggested that Martha join him or else return home.

"Go to the Sandwich Islands?" she wrote later. "With my Klondyke ticket bought, my passage booked, my vision of a million dollars in gold dust? Even after ten years of married life how little Will Purdy knew me!" This was the pivotal point of Martha's life. "The North

Star, my lodestar, beckoned me. It lured me onward. My whole being cried out to follow it. Miserable and heart-broken as I was, I could not turn back."

Will and Martha went their separate ways from then on. They never saw each other again. Divorce was very rare in those days. The thought of breaking up her marriage and carrying on alone was frightening for Martha. But once she had made the painful decision, she never looked back. She and Will were divorced two years later, and Will spent the rest of his life in Hawaii.

The company was dissolved and the boats sold. Although Eli and Sophy Gage made it as far as Alaska, they turned back without reaching Dawson.

Meanwhile, in Seattle, Martha was determined to continue on. George was horrified at the idea that his sister, whom he called Polly, was planning to go to the Yukon without her husband. But Martha pleaded with him to take her. Finally he agreed. They said nothing to their parents about the change of plans until they were well on their way.

6

HEADING NORTH

MARTHA was glad to leave the crowded hurly-burly of Seattle. On June 23, 1898, with George and Harry, she boarded a small steamer that would take them up the coast to Skagway, Alaska.

Many of the men slept wherever they could find an empty corner, but as one of the few women aboard, Martha wanted more privacy. She booked a berth in a stateroom at the enormous price of 120 dollars. To her surprise, she found herself sharing it with some of the more colourful characters on board. In the lower berth were "a tin-horn gambler and his female companion." In the upper berth was Birdie, who was heading north to work in one of the saloons, "destined to be one of the most notorious characters" of the Klondike. Sandwiched between them, in the middle berth, was an outraged Martha. Complaining to the captain was no help at all.

For someone from the protected life that Martha was used to, it was a shocking experience but, to her surprise, she soon felt completely at home. Her stateroom companions were friendly and kind. The gambler even brought her coffee in the mornings. The steamer itself was dirty and overloaded with passengers and freight. There were noisy parties every night. What a change it was from polite society in Chicago! But Martha found herself adapting to it quickly. Perhaps she even enjoyed seeing another way of life.

It took seven days for the steamer to wend its way up the West Coast as far as Skagway. Most of the trip was through the inland passage, weaving between the islands and the mountainous coast of British Columbia and Alaska. They were now so far north that it was never dark. Even at night there were only a few hours of twilight. Martha watched as huge icebergs drifted past the steamer. She saw schools of dolphins playing in the waves, and pods of beautiful black-and-white orca whales. White-capped mountains, carved by glaciers, rose from the shore. In the valleys between the mountains, Indian villages and totem poles could sometimes be seen.

In Skagway, ships from all over the world were depositing thousands of passengers onto the docks of what had been a tiny village only weeks before. There were men (and a very few women) who had come to seek a fortune in gold. There were others who planned to earn a living by providing services that the miners would need. But there were also those who had come to take advantage of the innocent among them, by robbing or cheating them.

By the time Martha, George and Harry arrived, Skagway was controlled by these criminals. The Americans provided no law enforcement in Skagway. The North-West Mounted Police officer, Sam Steele, called it the roughest place in the world. Bootleggers

Steele of the Mounted

By the fall of 1897, only about half of the four thousand or so stampeders who had arrived in Dawson made it back out before winter closed in. Those who remained were totally unprepared for the hunger and cold.

Early the following year, to protect the land for Canada, the Yukon was declared a territory, and the North-West Mounted Police, under Superintendent Sam Steele, immediately took steps to establish order.

To guard against another famine, Steele allowed no one to enter the territory without a year's supply of food. He sent his men to supervise the boat-building on the lakes along the trails, and had them assign a number to each new craft. The Mounties then checked that each boat arrived safely in Dawson. A search party was sent out to find those that didn't.

The constables under Steele were mostly from England. They were young, brave and polite. They settled arguments, gave advice and kept order.

By the summer of 1898, Dawson was firmly in the hands of the Mounties. The boys might be "whooping it up" in the saloons, but there was no shooting. In fact, there were few guns. Licences were required for revolvers, and very few were issued. Criminals were given one of two sentences. For minor offences, they were set to work on the Mounties' wood pile. For anything major, there was an escorted trip to the border. Gambling and prostitution were allowed, but Sunday was strictly observed. Everything shut down at midnight Saturday, and even fishing and cutting wood were forbidden. For a frontier town, it was extraordinarily peaceful and law-abiding.

and speakeasies sold illegal alcohol openly, and gambling joints regularly cheated their customers. Robbery and murder were a part of everyday life.

The steamer stopped in Skagway only long enough to unload supplies and travellers. From there, Martha, George and Harry pondered the next leg of their journey.

There were two ways to get to Bennett Lake, where the way to Dawson continued by water. The White Pass Trail started in Skagway. It was favoured by some, since pack animals could be used to carry supplies up it. But it was a longer route than the Chilkoot Pass Trail, and it was fairly new and in poor condition. So many horses and mules died along its path that it came to be known as Dead Horse Trail.

They decided to continue on by boat to Dyea. From here, George decided that the Chilkoot was the best one for their party.

The Chilkoot was an ancient trail that had been used by generations of Tlingits who controlled trade between the coast and the interior. Only a year earlier, Dyea had been an empty beach near a native Tlingit village and a trading post. By the time Martha arrived, a town of small, rough wooden buildings (with false fronts to make them look more impressive) had sprung up. There were restaurants, bars and hotels, as well as stores where the stampeders could buy almost anything.

The Tlingit continued to control the pass to a certain extent, and both men and women acted as packers for the gold rushers. Their fee of a thousand dollars was a huge sum at the time, but the gold rush was quickly inflating prices. Those who couldn't afford the fee faced

No one was allowed into the Yukon without enough supplies to last through one winter. This is a typical list of the goods that had to be carried in for one person:

400 lbs flour	1 lb pepper	50 lbs evaporated potatoes
50 lbs cornmeal	1/2 lb mustard	24 lbs coffee
50 lbs oatmeal	1/4 lb ginger	5 lbs tea
35 lbs rice	25 lbs evaporated apples	4 doz. tins condensed milk
100 lbs beans	25 lbs evaporated peaches	5 bars laundry soap
40 lbs candles	25 lbs evaporated apricots	60 boxes matches
100 lbs granulated sugar	25 lbs fish	15 lbs soup vegetables
8 lbs baking powder	10 lbs pitted plums	25 cans butter
200 lbs bacon	50 lbs evaporated onions	
2 lbs soda		
36 yeast cakes		
15 lbs salt		

The beach at Dyea where Martha and the other stampeders unloaded their goods and belongings before heading up the Chilkoot Pass Trail.

a discouraging task. While the Tlingit usually carried a hundred pounds in one trip, most stampeders could manage only about fifty. On their own, they might take three months to transfer their supplies across the pass.

George was able to arrange to have their goods (several tons of them) packed in for nine hundred dollars.

As she watched the little steamer leave Dyea, Martha had a sinking feeling. She was now cut off completely from her old life, but she quickly reminded herself of the heroic ancestors she had admired as a child and tried to face the future with a cheerful heart.

They stayed in Dyea for two weeks. The men camped out in tents, but a friendly resident let Martha use his shanty while he bunked with a neighbour. Martha enjoyed her stay there. The compact little shack had a stove, two chairs, a table and a bunk. She spent her time fishing, practising hiking on the mountain trails, and cooking and washing up for the others. She was thrilled by all the wildflowers, and she wrote of the fields of wild blue iris and the lupins she knew from home. The beauty of the landscape touched her deeply, but she was lonely for her children. Not a day passed, she wrote to her parents, when "we do not speak of you or think of you. Kiss my babies, love them, cherish them, as I know you will."

7

CONQUERING THE CHILKOOT PASS

O N July 12, 1898, Martha, George and Harry took their place among the hundreds of others starting out along the trail to the forbidding Chilkoot Pass. They were a strange sight. Martha in her stylish costume, sporting a sturdy stick to help her over the rocky ground, was surrounded by roughly clad men with heavy packs on their backs. Some had their supplies piled on sleighs or carts pulled by horses or even dogs. Some drove herds of pack ponies, a few were leading cows, and one woman drove an oxcart.

The route from Dyea to Dawson was more than 700 kilometres (430 miles). Most of it could be travelled by boat, but only after hiking in from the coast to the mountains, then up and over the Chilkoot Pass, a distance of nearly 60 kilometres (40 miles).

At first the trail was a pleasant walk along a wagon road, but soon Martha was stepping from rock to rock across the swift mountain streams. She climbed over enormous boulders and through the tangled roots of fallen trees in her long and bulky skirt.

The scenery was wild and beautiful, but everywhere

there were signs of just how dangerous the trail was. It was littered with the discarded belongings of stampeders who were attempting to lighten their loads, or who had given up and turned back. On either side of the trail, Martha was horrified to see the rotting bodies of horses that had fallen along the way. Once she picked up a baby's bootee from the snow and ice, and wondered sadly what tragic story it might tell.

Even without a heavy pack to carry, Martha found the climb almost unbearable. Her feet were soon sore and blistered. Her face was covered with mosquito bites. Her hands were torn and scraped. They stopped once for a welcome break at a small cabin, where a widow and her son served them tea and sandwiches. Then they continued on.

At last they reached Sheep Camp, named for the mountain sheep that inhabited the surrounding peaks.

Sheep Camp on the Chilkoot Trail. Beyond here there were no trees—only rocky, glacier-studded mountains.

Here they planned to spend their first night.

Sheep Camp was a makeshift village of tents and small shacks that were called hotels. Martha and George found room in one of them, the impressively named Grand Pacific Hotel. Look at your woodshed if you want to know what it is like, Martha wrote to her parents. As one of the few women on the trail, she was well treated and given a partitioned corner of the cabin for the night. In the morning there was a hearty breakfast, and she was presented with the last orange in the camp.

Sheep Camp lay at the base of the mountains. This was as far as the animals could travel. Ahead lay a narrow path that seemed to lead straight up over ice-covered rock. Just three months before, an avalanche had swept across the trail, burying hundreds of climbers and leaving sixty dead. Now it was time for Martha to begin the climb.

The mountain tops and high passes were covered by glaciers even at the height of summer, and the hot, July sun had turned the heavily travelled snow to ice. As they climbed, the trail became steeper and narrower. Martha clutched at jutting rocks and the twisted roots of the few stunted trees that grew at this height. Ahead she saw the narrow trail, now barely wide enough for one foot at a time. To her left rose the steep side of the mountain. To her right the cliff dropped away to a frightening abyss. She cursed her high collar, the tight, heavy corset, the long corduroy skirt and the full bloomers. (She could neither wear nor pack the straw hat, and George ended up carrying it over the pass on the end of his staff!)

"Mush on. Mush on." Over and over Martha repeated to herself the stampeders' cry of encouragement. The

Women in the Klondike

While tens of thousands of men flooded into the Klondike in 1897 and 1898, only a few thousand women made the trip. They were unusual women for their time.

At the end of the nineteenth century, most women in Europe and North America were only beginning to demand some of the rights and freedoms that men had. Their movements were restricted. They were thought to be too delicate for strenuous activity (although those at the lower level of society were required to work very hard). The only paid work open to them was nursing, teaching or, in a few cases, secretarial jobs. Many longed for adventure.

When the gold rush was at its height, women were being warned that the trails were no place for them. A Seattle paper went so far as to say that it was impossible for a woman to survive the passes. But, like Martha, many did make it, some of them with small children. What they lacked in strength, they made up for with perseverance.

They came to the Yukon for a variety of reasons. Some hoped to make a fortune. Some accompanied their husbands. Some came to save souls or nurse the sick. Others travelled as tourists or simply for the adventure. A surprising number came as journalists.

The women who came to the Yukon usually ended up making a living not from the gold fields directly, but from starting businesses or doing the kind of entertaining, cooking, sewing and washing that they had done back home. For most of them, it was a thrilling experience, and it proved that they were capable of much more than was expected of women at the time.

E.A. Hegg

Some of the most compelling photographs of Canada's history were taken during the Yukon gold rush. Of these, the most remarkable are those taken by E.A. Hegg.

Eric Hegg was born in Sweden. He was just twenty-nine years old and working out of his own photographic studio in Bellingham Bay, Washington State, when news of the discovery of gold in the Yukon hit the outside world. He saw at once that this was a wonderful opportunity for a photographer. He closed his studio, bought all the materials he could afford, and headed north.

Hegg must have made an interesting picture himself as he travelled along the trail with a team of goats pulling the sled that carried his portable darkroom. He had to make all kinds of makeshift arrangements to keep his materials from freezing.

By the summer of 1898, he had set up a studio in a log shack in Dawson, where he continued to record the history of the gold rush. His pictures of the agonies of the trail, of the crowded scenes at the temporary tent cities set up along the way, and especially those of the incredible climb over the Chilkoot Pass have kept the Klondike story vividly alive ever since.

last hundred paces rose before her. She was weak with fatigue. Every muscle screamed out for rest, but the thin line of climbers in front of her kept moving up the mountain while hundreds more pressed forward from behind.

"Cheer up, Polly!" George called back to her, just as she felt she could go no farther. "Only one hundred feet to go now."

This photograph shows how difficult the climb was at the steepest part of the pass.

The other men in the group turned to give her a hand over the most strenuous and terrifying section of the trail. "Don't look down," they warned her. Then, with only a few steps to go, Martha's foot was caught in a jagged hole in the trail. A sharp, protruding rock tore through her leather boot and left her foot throbbing. She fell to the side of the path weeping with pain. The line of climbing men continued on, moving past her.

George gradually managed to work his way back to help her but, knowing that their goal was so close, his patience soon ran out. "For God's sake, Polly, buck up and be a man!" he cried out in frustration. Martha could hard-

The North-West Mounted Police station at the very top of the pass. Here the climbers entered Canada for the first time.

ly bear the pain, but she wasn't going to let George get the best of her! She pulled herself to her feet, forced the aches and pains to the back of her mind, and joined the line once more. Soon she was walking over the summit.

The top of the pass was bitterly cold and swept by an icy wind. Martha longed to be warm and to rest, and George, who was beginning to worry about her, rewarded her with a five-dollar fire—one whole luxurious hour of heat. While it burned, she dried her socks and dabbed her cuts and scrapes with iodine.

Suddenly all her pain and misery disappeared, and Martha was flushed with a feeling of triumph. She had done it! She had accomplished what even many men had found impossible. She was on her way to the Klondike, where gold was waiting for anyone who could survive the lengthy and dangerous trip.

After a bracing cup of tea, Martha and George entered Canada for the first time. Here the North-West Mounted Police had their customs shed, where they collected duties and stopped criminals from entering the country. Martha was impressed by the Mounties and thought that "finer, sturdier, more intelligent-looking men would be hard to find." Unlike Skagway, here the law was strictly enforced.

The most rigorous part of the trail was now behind them, but there were still many challenges to come before Martha and George reached Dawson City. Descending the mountain seemed even more difficult than climbing it. The path plunged through a rocky forest. Martha called it a "hideous nightmare." She tripped over roots and scraped her hands and knees on rocks. Her boots were torn to shreds. Finally she begged the men to just leave her and let her lie down beside the trail. Then George put an arm around her waist. She leaned on him, and together they walked the last stretch.

When they reached the village of Lindeman, Martha sank gratefully onto the bed George had rented in one of the makeshift hotels. It was just a piece of canvas stretched across four logs, with a straw mattress, but to Martha it was the softest bed in the world. As she drifted off to sleep, a feeling of pride surged through her. She had actually made it over the Chilkoot Pass! "I would never do it again....Not for all the gold in the Klondike," she wrote. "And yet, knowing now what it meant, would I miss it? ... No, never! ... Not even for all the gold in the world!"

Martha's view from the bitterly cold summit of the pass.

8

MUSHING ON TO DAWSON

THE supplies that George, Harry and Martha were having carried in to Lindeman were slow making their way over the pass, and they had to wait for the boat they were having built to take them the rest of the way to Dawson. It was just as well. They all needed a rest. Martha was happy to relax, to cook for their small group, and to study the plant life that lay around her.

She recognized many of the wildflowers from home. Forget-me-nots, Dutchman's breeches and wild bleeding hearts bloomed in profusion. She was fascinated by a northern relative of the Venus flytrap, and watched for hours as its deadly flower captured the midges that filled the warm summer air.

At first they slept outside on beds of straw, but soon two cabins were passed on to them by a group of Australian stampeders who were moving on. "Just turn them over to someone else when you are finished with them," they said in parting.

One cabin was a large one with a huge fireplace. At night some of the other campers would gather around it

LINDEMAN.

The tent city at Lindeman where Martha, George and Harry rested from their climb.

for warmth and company. When the baggage finally arrived, they passed the long evenings with George playing his mandolin and Martha her guitar, while everyone joined in singing hymns and popular songs.

Then their boat was ready, and Martha, George and Harry, along with their navigator Captain Spencer and two others, loaded up their goods and set off by sail across Bennett Lake to Caribou Crossing (Carcross). They spent the night there, and Martha had to deal with wet wood as she tried to cook for the group over a smoky campfire. The next morning they sailed through Windy Arm—almost too windy for them to navigate—and down Lake Tagish to land at a Mountie post.

Here all the boats were checked for liquor. It was only later that Martha was told why the men had insisted that she rest on a couple of boxes covered with blankets. That was where the whisky had been stored!

More than eighteen thousand travellers had passed through the post since May of the previous year, and Martha was only the 631st woman. Each boat was numbered as it passed. Theirs was number 14,405.

They continued on. When they reached the Yukon River, they had to pass through Miles Canyon and the White Horse Rapids. The year before, hundreds of boats had been wrecked in this stretch. Then the Mounties took over. They made sure the boats were judged to be

At the height of the summer of 1898, Lake Laberge was full of ships of all sorts and sizes making the long trip to Dawson. The one Martha and her companions had built was shaped like a fisherman's dory. It could barely float when they and their seven tons of supplies had been loaded in, but they sailed bravely across the lake with the others.

safe before they were allowed to continue past this point. All boats had to be steered by competent men, and no women or children were allowed to undertake the trip— they had to walk along the grassy bank. Nonetheless, a few adventurous women did brave the rapids secretly, risking a hundred-dollar fine if they were caught. Among them was Martha.

As the river descended into the canyon, it was forced into a deep and narrow channel. The water foamed and raced. Steep cliffs rose on either side. They travelled swiftly through, evading the crushing force of the powerful whirlpool at its centre, and entered the White Horse Rapids, named for the foam that billowed up like the manes of prancing horses. Here the boat's steering oar snapped in two, but the fast action of Captain Spencer, who seized another oar and gave quick directions to the men, saw them safely through.

From here they still had ten days to travel before they would reach Dawson, but the most dangerous part of the trip was over. Each day they spent eight hours sailing. Sometimes the wind blew them along. Sometimes they had to row, and sometimes they just drifted with the current. They travelled the length of Lake Laberge, through Five Finger Rapids, and gradually the river became wider and smoother.

During the long northern evenings they camped, fished for trout or whitefish, hunted squirrels (which Martha could only eat after days of doing without meat of any kind), gathered berries and made their beds under the stars. When it rained, they took shelter in the tents. They stayed up late in the light-filled evenings, often singing with others who were camped nearby.

Sourdoughs and Cheechakos

Yukon inhabitants came to be known as either "sourdoughs" or "cheechakos."

Cheechako was a Native word meaning an inexperienced newcomer. It originally referred to anyone who came to the Yukon after the winter of 1898-99. Later it was used for those who had never spent a full winter there. The oldtimers were called sourdoughs, an essential recipe for pioneers.

Sourdough is a fermented dough that was used to make bread, biscuits and flapjacks in the Yukon. In almost every cabin, a pail of sourdough hung over the iron stove. Pioneers guarded their sourdough "starter" (a bit of dough saved from an earlier batch), which got better and better with use.

At Lindeman, Martha learned how to make sourdough. This is her recipe:

"Mix a thin batter of flour and water. Add a little rice or macaroni water and a pinch of sugar. Put mixture in a pail, cover it and hang over the stove, keeping it warm for four hours."

It was a pleasant time, but a far cry from the life Martha had been used to in Chicago. The only drawbacks were the hordes of mosquitoes that persecuted them all along the route ("bloodthirsty brutes" Martha called them), but they soon learned to make their camp on high ground to escape most of them.

All along the way, other stampeders sailed in front, beside and behind them. Groups were always camped nearby at the end of the day. They came from all over the world. Martha and George met many people, and some of those who ended up staying in the Yukon remained friends for life.

One evening, two days before they reached Dawson, they were camping near a group of men from New Zealand. Martha invited them for a special dinner— hardtack (a kind of biscuit), coffee and dried apple dumplings. The New Zealanders called it their "best meal since leaving home."

Twelve days after setting sail, they rounded a bend in the calm river and saw Dawson. It was August 5, 1898.

9

THE LITTLE CHEECHAKO

❦

THE cheechakos had been pouring into Dawson since early June. Only two months before Martha arrived, it had been a small town of about two thousand people who had made it over the trails the previous summer. Since then some thirty thousand newcomers had flooded in, making it larger than either Vancouver or Victoria, and only slightly smaller than Winnipeg, then the biggest city in the Canadian West.

The first priority was to find somewhere to live. Land and building supplies had become wildly expensive. Martha and the men soon found that the cheapest place was across the Klondike River, in Klondike City, known to one and all as Lousetown. Here they could squat, without paying for the land.

The men got quickly to work and built a cabin on a hill above the town. There was a partitioned corner for Martha and bunks built into the walls for themselves. Their packing boxes became a cupboard and dressing table. They made bent-willow chairs. The table was two boards nailed to tree-trunk legs.

Martha began at once to turn the rough cabin into a home. First she nailed blankets to the inside walls to make it cosier. She had brought along some of the comforts of home, including two linen tablecloths and two dozen table napkins, a set of silver knives and forks, and a whole bolt of sage-green cloth with roses on it. With the cloth she made curtains, pillows (stuffed with feathers from wild ducks) and covers for the boxes and cupboards. A piece of colourful oilcloth brightened up the table and, for the wildflowers she loved to gather, she made a vase by covering a tin with birchbark.

Dawson was now a booming city in almost every respect. It had two newspapers, two banks, a telegraph office, telephones and five churches. But it was also a city of muddy streets and canvas houses.

Most things were paid for in gold dust. It sifted out of the seams of the cloth "pokes" or sacks the miners carried and collected like ordinary dust in the cracks of the floors. Some people were making quick fortunes, but most were spending their money just as quickly. Almost everything was available for sale, but prices were roughly one hundred times what they were down south. Fresh food of any kind was particularly expensive. Eggs were considered a special treat and were as valuable as the gold itself.

There were up to thirty thousand people milling around Dawson at any one time that summer. Many of them were searching for a friend, a relative or a travelling companion. But there were no addresses in this instant city. The only way to make contact was through a note on one of the general notice boards.

As soon as Martha had made all the improvements to

Using the wide, shallow bowls shown here, prospectors panned for gold by shaking the gold-bearing mix they had scooped from the streams, while pouring the water and gravel out. The gold, being heavier, sank to the bottom of the pan and was collected.

Before long the miners were shifting streams to flow down a sluice (an artificial channel made of boards like the one the men are standing in here), separating the gold from the stones and gravel more quickly. Within a few years, large companies moved in and, working with giant dredges, sifted the gold out mechanically.

their new home that she could, she started to try to track down William Lambert's fortune, so she could claim her share. But Dawson had grown too quickly for government services to serve people efficiently. The offices were confused and disorganized, and the people who worked there were often corrupt. When Martha approached the Gold Commissioner's office to try to trace the claim, she found that the records had frequently been scratched out and written over, or sometimes cut out completely and replaced with something new. Everyone had to be bribed. The registered letters she sent in an attempt to trace the witnesses to the will often disappeared into thin air. As Martha put it, she "went on and on, tipping and tipping until money was getting perilously low." But the Lamberts and all trace of them had disappeared.

Soon Martha had to face up to a much more serious situation. Not only had she conquered the dreadful Chilkoot Pass, but she had done so while pregnant! She had ignored her suspicions as long as possible but, by fall, she could do so no longer. She and her companions had planned to return south before freeze-up, but Martha knew she could never make it over the pass now. The thought of spending the winter in the Yukon terrified her.

Finally she told George that she was going to have a baby. He was horrified. "I never should have consented to your coming," he responded. "Father will never forgive me." Their cousin, Harry, left before winter and took the news home with him. "By this time Martha is dead," he told his family. "She was going to have a baby, and she couldn't possibly live, she looked so ill."

But hardship brought out the best in Martha. She began to make preparations for the new baby. The table linens she had brought with her were turned into diapers and nightgowns. Then the long northern nights set in. For weeks there was no sign of the sun. By day she cooked and kept house for the men. In the evenings she sewed or played cards with the others. When American Thanksgiving and then Christmas arrived, they celebrated with baked stuffed ptarmigan, canned corn and popcorn balls.

There were times of terror and loneliness, too. She was alone with the men, living in primitive conditions—no running water, no electricity, none of the help that she had always been used to. There was no one to share her fears with. It was bitterly cold, and dark both night and day.

She wrote home constantly, but little mail made it through from the south. She missed her children and her parents. She could no longer bear to look at their pictures, so she hid them away. "I look back now and wonder how I got through the months of mental anguish in 1898, before my baby was born," she later wrote. "Night after night I prayed to die."

She spoke to Father Judge, a Jesuit missionary known as the Saint of Dawson for the dedicated care he gave the sick in his hospital. But it would cost a thousand dollars to have her baby there, and her money was gone. Father Judge would give her credit until she could pay, but Martha had never owed money to anyone and couldn't face doing so now.

On January 31, the men went off to work their gold claims as usual. Martha was alone in the cabin all day. To

The cabin built on the hill above Lousetown. This is where Martha spent her first winter in the Yukon.

Martha, Lyman and George in February, 1899, inside their cabin. The walls are hung with blankets, and the furniture is covered with the flowered fabric that they had carried over the Chilkoot Trail.

their astonishment, when they returned at the end of the day, she was lying in bed holding a new baby boy wrapped in red flannel. She called it an incredibly easy birth!

Although Martha made light of the experience in later years, that she was able to deliver her own baby and that he survived with no ill effects is amazing. She named the baby Lyman after her grandfather, but to the men he was the little cheechako.

10

THE YUKON BECOMES HOME

NEW baby in a community that had few women or children was exciting for everyone. The men in the cabin took charge of cooking and cleaning. George gave the little cheechako his first bath. ("He nearly passed out," Martha recalled.) The prospectors came to see the infant and brought treats they had been saving for a special event—moose meat, chocolate, olive oil, fresh bread and, of course, gold dust and gold nuggets.

Little Lyman was an instant hit. The cabin became a community centre for the lonely men. They loved to have a chance to hold the baby. They stayed on to talk and to sing, with George and Martha playing the mandolin and the guitar.

It was lonely for Martha without any women to talk to about the problems of feeding the men and caring for the baby. For most of the winter, she was alone in the cabin with little Lyman all day.

It was a long and hard winter. The temperature dropped to minus fifty. Disease ran through Dawson—typhoid, malaria and dysentery. In spite of the steps

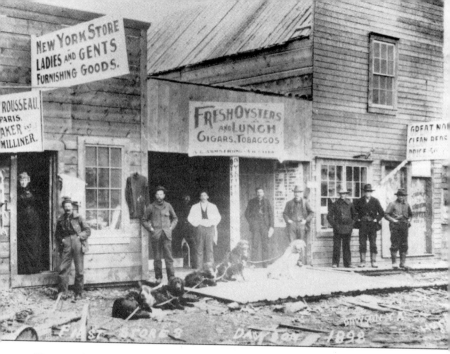

Dawson's main street.

Sam Steele had taken to make sure that newcomers arrived with supplies, food ran low. For six months, Martha and the men had no butter, sugar or milk. Cornmeal mush, a boiled porridge of water and corn-meal, was a basic. Fresh fruit and vegetables were impossible to come by.

On April 26 a devastating fire tore through Dawson. It was still far from spring. The temperature that night was minus forty-five. The whole of the downtown—one hundred and seventeen buildings—went up in flames. Martha and Lyman were safely on the other side of the Klondike River, but the fire was clearly visible from their home. It reminded Martha vividly of the fire from her childhood.

As soon as the fire had burned itself out, a different

kind of gold rush was underway. The streets and building sites themselves were panned for gold that had seeped out of the pokes and through the floorboards. Then the rebuilding of Dawson began. New stores and dance halls took the place of the old. But instead of muddy streets and rough pioneer buildings, there were sidewalks, a sewer system, schools and sturdy houses.

Another crisis, this time closer to home, struck almost a month later, on May 23. It was a beautiful sunny day and Martha had taken Lyman outside, where he was swaying in a swing made from a condensed milk box. The spring blossoms of the Yukon's pasque flower dotted the landscape with purple.

Suddenly a low, rumbling sound startled Martha. Thinking that this might finally be her chance to shoot a bear, she quickly moved Lyman to safety in the cabin and returned, well prepared with two rifles, two revolvers and a shotgun! She thought she was ready for anything.

Then, raising her eyes to the hill behind the house, she saw to her horror that the whole slope had turned into a giant landslide. It was heading straight towards the house.

She ran back into the cabin, bundled up the baby and braced herself in one corner of the room. Miraculously, the slide struck a secure clump of trees just above the building, splitting into two streams that smashed past either side of the cabin. Martha collapsed onto the bed with Lyman held tightly in her arms.

When she came to her senses, she heard another extraordinary sound. It was the ice in the Yukon River, breaking up with a roar. Spring had come, and Martha had survived a full winter.

She was no longer a cheechako; she was now a sour-dough.

Martha had told her parents back home in Kansas nothing of the expected baby, and Harry's family hadn't let them know, either. In February she finally wrote to give them the news. Her father left for the Yukon as soon as he could. Before the end of July, to Martha's surprise, he walked in the cabin door. He had come to take her and the baby back home. She would rejoin her other sons and live with her mother and father on the ranch.

Martha left the Yukon very unwillingly. Throughout the warm early days of summer, she had learned to love the country and her life there. Her wildflower collection was growing, fresh food had arrived with the early boats, and she still hoped to earn her fortune. While on their way to Dawson, she and George, like everyone else on

---

A Special Meal

When Martha's father arrived at the end of July in 1899, Martha and George decided to celebrate with an especially delicious meal. They had been eating dried vegetables, powdered soup and cornmeal all winter.

A load of fresh food had just arrived from the south. Only one onion and one potato were allowed to each family, and they cost a dollar each.

This was the menu for the memorable feast:

1/2 pound of moose liver fried with bacon
1 onion, sliced and fried
1 huge potato, baked
brown bread without butter
tea without sugar
rice and molasses

---

the trail, had staked claims. Theirs were on Excelsior Creek, a stream named by Martha.

In the end she agreed to go, leaving the claims in the hands of George. She promised to give up her dream of returning to the Yukon if the claims did not produce gold.

The return trip, while still hazardous, was far different from the journey only a year earlier. By now the White Pass Railway line had been blasted through the rocky trail. It took Martha, Lyman and her father only hours to travel in comfort through the pass to Skagway, instead of the two agonizing days of the climb the year before.

Back in Kansas, Martha was delighted to be together with her three children at her parents' beautiful tree-filled ranch. Warren was now eleven and Donald about seven. Fresh fruits and vegetables, such a luxury in the North, grew here in abundance.

It was a happy summer, but Martha's happiness was short-lived. She was now thirty-three. As winter descended, there was little for her to do. Her children were well cared for by others. They were at home with their grandparents and didn't seem to need her. She felt that she had failed as both a wife and mother, and in her quest for a fortune. She fell into a depression.

Finally she shook herself out of her sadness with thoughts of the Klondike. The lure of the North began to work its magic again. She felt that her destiny lay there. In June she heard from George that there was gold in the land they had staked. She immediately made plans to return, this time with Warren, who was now twelve.

Before she left, Martha began making practical plans

for the future, with her father's help. It was decided that she would set up a saw mill in the Yukon. She and Warren were to go ahead and get settled. Her father, her mother and the two boys would follow the next year with the machinery that the mill would require.

Everything got underway according to plan. Martha and Warren headed north. With two partners she formed a company to work the claims, and they set up a mining camp at Excelsior Creek, just outside Dawson. They built a storehouse, a cabin for Martha and a bunkhouse for the crew of sixteen.

For the next year Martha took care of Warren and cooked and cleaned for the men. It was a hard year, but she enjoyed it, working all day and, at night, reading or writing in the journal that she would continue to keep for the rest of her life.

In the spring of 1901 the whole family arrived, along with everything needed for the mill. A large plot of land was bought near Dawson. A six-room cabin called Mill Lodge was built, along with a number of one-room cabins. The family stayed for a year and then left, taking Warren with them. He was to live with his grandfather Purdy and continue his education. Martha was left alone in charge of the mill with little Lyman and nine-year-old Donald.

Spending the year with his mother at the Yukon lumber mill was an exciting time for Donald. During the school term he went to the Dawson public school. At night he did his homework under his mother's sharp eyes.

But this was the frontier. There was always something interesting to see and do on the banks of the Klondike River. And the mill itself, where the logs were turned into neat piles of lumber, was a fascinating place.

Donald was a serious boy and eager to help around the mill. But as spring arrived, Martha began to realize that something was wrong.

At that time, it was very unusual for a woman to be in charge of a business—especially in the Yukon. The men, with the encouragement of the foreman, complained about being "run by a skirt." The precious tools needed to keep the mill in good shape were being misplaced or mysteriously lost. Martha began to suspect that someone was deliberately trying to undermine the work.

She asked Donald to check every night to see that the tools were safely stored. He enjoyed having the responsibility—his very own job just before bed each night. But one day Martha again found tools lying about late at night. The next morning she spoke to Donald about being more careful. "I have always put everything away at night," he said, "but sometimes lately I have had to put lots of tools away twice."

Martha knew then that something was seriously wrong. With great courage, and in spite of the fact that logs were arriving daily and orders for lumber were pouring in, she faced the crew with what she knew and paid them off.

It was the height of the lumber season. Her crew was gone. Martha, exhausted from the hard work and totally discouraged, was wondering what to do when Donald touched her shoulder. "Never mind, Mother," he said. "I'll work for you."

The touching support from her small son gave her the strength that she needed. With the help of the Mounties, Martha soon had another, more reliable crew

FRONT STREET DAWSON JULY 4 '99 POLE VAULTING CONTEST WON BY H. WAKE

Dawson was an unusual city in many ways. For one thing, it was a Canadian city in a Canadian territory, but most of its residents were citizens of the United States. There was some concern over this as the two national holidays approached—Canada's Dominion Day on July 1 and the American celebration on July 4. But the Mounties eased the tension by deciding that festivities would be held for both days. In fact, it turned into a five-day celebration. "Canadians are seemingly as delighted to help us celebrate our national holiday as we were to join them on Dominion Day..." Martha wrote home to her parents, "10,000 Americans and Canadians paraded up and down singing alternately 'My Country 'tis of Thee' and 'God Save the Queen.'" They played baseball, the sourdoughs against the cheechakos. They had fireworks but, Martha wrote, "the beautiful colour effect was lost entirely in the daylight."

Gold Rush Pioneer 69

operating the mill. She ran it successfully until the fall of 1904, when a chance meeting changed her life once more.

11

MRS. GEORGE BLACK

MARTHA'S early claims along the Excelsior River had paid off handsomely but, like most of the stampeders, she invested her earnings in other claims and ended up with nothing. Now it was her business ability that kept the family going. Donald and Lyman were living with her in Mill Lodge. Warren was living with Will's father and studying in the United States, a decision Martha later regretted, since Warren never returned to live in the Yukon.

By 1901 half of those who had flocked to Dawson in 1898 were gone. The city began to become a more settled community. There were no more wild celebrations where thousands of dollars changed hands in a single night. The men and women who stayed on to make Dawson their home wanted a more normal city. The "upper class" of Dawson began to follow the customs they had been used to in the south. Social conventions such as invitations to tea became common. There were dances, skating parties, card parties and tennis in the summer.

Dawson's once free-wheeling society became much

more structured. At the top were government officials, Mountie officers, successful businessmen and heads of religion. Then came the less successful businessmen. Next were the Mountie constables, the mine workers and the laborers and, below them, the men who were part Native or had Native wives, and the dance-hall girls and prostitutes. The Natives, the original inhabitants of the Yukon, were at the very bottom. Most of them lived on the nearby Moosehide reserve.

Martha fitted in everywhere. As a woman of society, she was welcomed at the highest levels. As a successful businesswoman, she was part of the business community. But she was also friendly with the men and women at the lower end of the social scale, many of whom worked for her or were her customers. They came to her when they needed help, and she always had a meal for anyone who turned up at her door hungry. In *I Married the Klondike*, Laura Beatrice Berton described Martha as "a pretty, saucy-faced woman with steel-blue eyes and an expression of unqualified determination.... I decided, as we chatted, that in spite of her mobile lips she would be a hard woman to cross, and when I later learned her story I knew I was right."

Martha's financial success meant that she was able to buy new furniture for Mill Lodge from the Simpson's and Eaton's catalogues. She bought a Paris gown every year. As one of the few single women in the community, she often had the chance to marry. One of her proposals was from George Black, a Dawson lawyer.

George had grown up in New Brunswick. He, too, had been swept up in the excitement of the gold rush and had spent two years prospecting and mining in the

Yukon before settling down to practise law in Dawson. Martha met him when she went to get advice on a legal problem in 1902. They were immediately attracted to each other, and within two weeks George had proposed.

Martha was reluctant to marry. She was happy with her life at the mill. She liked being independent. George was seven years younger than she was, and perhaps that made her hesitate, too. But she and George had many happy times over the next two years. They both loved nature and the outdoors, and Martha admired George's interest in politics and his desire to do as much as he could for the Yukon. And the interest he took in her sons won her heart.

Finally, in the summer of 1904, they were married at Mill Lodge. Martha wore an elegant pearl-grey gown trimmed with pink silk, and she carried a muff of pink roses. The outfit was topped off with a hat of more pink roses. The muff and hat had small coloured birds peeking out of them. Describing it later, Martha admitted that the outfit sounded ridiculous, but insisted that it was "very swanky" at the time. She still loved to dress up, and the wedding was a good excuse for going all out.

Martha, George, Donald and Lyman moved into George's house in Dawson. As usual, Martha threw herself into her new role. She gave up the mill and quickly adopted all of her new husband's interests. She became an Anglican, a Conservative and a passionate supporter of the British Empire.

George loved the outdoors. He took a keen interest in birds and all of nature, and he was an enthusiastic photographer, hunter and fisherman. Many mornings the whole family crawled out of their warm beds before daylight to watch the miracle of the spring migration. Birds of every kind passed over Dawson on their way to their northern breeding grounds. First came the geese, ducks, swans and cranes; then the waders and plovers; finally the warblers, thrushes, swallows, hummingbirds and

One of Martha Black's carefully collected and mounted Yukon wildflowers. The pasque flower was one of her favourites and was once chosen as the territory's official flower. In more recent years, it has been replaced by the fireweed.

multitudes of others. The chickadees, buntings and woodpeckers stayed all year round, as did the huge, playful black ravens.

George's interests fitted perfectly with Martha's love of collecting and studying wildflowers. Their camping and hiking trips gave her many opportunities to add to her growing knowledge of native plants. At that time, little had been recorded about the natural world in the North, and Martha was one of the region's early naturalists.

As time went by, Martha's interest in the wildflowers of the Yukon became more widely known. She was invited to speak to clubs and other gatherings on the subject. She began mounting and displaying the plants and flowers she had collected to use in her talks. She created what she called "artistic botany," something she became quite famous for over the years. She would carefully press and dry the flowers, using absorbent cotton to separate the petals or to preserve their shape, then mount them on paper that she had painted with watercolours.

When the Yukon government announced a prize of two hundred dollars for the best exhibit of native wildflowers, Martha began an ambitious project. She had three objectives: to show as many varieties as possible, to stress the scientific side by mounting whole plants, including roots, and to show the kinds of artistic arrangements that were possible. Her display included 464 varieties of plants. Many of the local people helped her, from small children searching out unusual species, to the miners who arrived at her door with rare and delicate plants.

Of course Martha won the prize. Her elaborate exhibit was sent to the Seattle World's Fair, where it surprised many who thought of the Yukon as cold and barren with little in the way of plant life.

In 1909, the family moved to Vancouver, planning to stay for a year while George took the law exams in British Columbia. With fewer and fewer people in Dawson, he needed to expand his practice. Here Martha's work with wildflowers became known through the pressed flower place cards she used at her dinner parties. One of her guests, a woman responsible for decorating the Canadian Pacific hotels, had the idea of using native flowers in the hotels. Martha was hired to put together displays of B.C. flowers for the CPR.

The boys, now ten and seventeen, went off happily to spend the summer on a friend's farm in northern Ontario. Martha was given a wonderful personal trip through the Fraser River valley by rail in order to collect her flowers. She could ask the train to stop whenever she saw a likely patch of flowers. Violets, harebells, spring beauties, campions and orchids grew in abundance. She collected butterflies to add to the display. She rode up mountain trails on horseback and camped under the stars. She wandered the tracks alone, meeting railway workers and baggage men and wanderers of the road. They were all helpful. When she was ready to move on, she tied a white cloth to a stick, stuck it in the ground between the tracks and waited to be picked up. It was one of the happiest summers of her life.

Her displays were so successful that she was invited by the government of Belgium to travel to that country and spend three years making a collection of their native plants. She was tempted to go but, in the end, thought that she couldn't leave the family for so long. Eventually her B.C. collection was put on permanent display in the Parliament Buildings in Victoria, where it remained for many years.

The Poet of the Yukon

Although Robert Service is one of the best-known figures connected with the Yukon gold rush, he didn't arrive until 1904, long after the excitement was over. Martha first met the man she described as a "dreamy modest Scottish bank clerk" when he turned up at a carnival as one of the Gold Dust Twins.

Service's poems, such as "The Shooting of Dan McGrew" and "The Cremation of Sam McGee," were wildly romantic and inaccurate. But they captured the spirit of the period for many outside the territory. His first book, *Songs of a Sourdough*, has sold more than three million copies over the years.

12

WAR!

To Martha's delight, the family was able to move back to Dawson in 1912. During the election of 1911, George had worked hard to help Robert Borden's Conservative government replace Wilfrid Laurier's Liberals. As a reward, he was now appointed Commissioner of the Territory, with responsibilities similar to those of the premier of a province.

The Blacks arrived home by way of what Martha called the longest stage journey in the world, almost 650 kilometres (400 miles). The trip from Whitehorse to Dawson took ten days by sleigh, with stops to change horses and nights spent in roadhouse bunks.

By now fewer than three thousand people lived in Dawson. As George's wife, Martha was the "first lady" of the Yukon. Years later she said, "My first home was a one-room log cabin and my last home was Government House. I was just as happy in one as in the other."

Martha loved to entertain, and she felt strongly that receptions at Government House should be open to all levels of society. For their first reception, she had a thousand sandwiches, twenty gallons of sherbet and gallons

Flowers remained an important part of Martha's life no matter where she was. Here she is in Dawson in 1915, wife of the Yukon Commissioner, delivering flowers from her garden with a Mountie escort.

of punch prepared, and let it be known that everyone was welcome. Six hundred people came and stayed until five in the morning. Another time she shocked half the town by inviting an old friend of George's to a reception, along with his wife, who had been known as Diamond Tooth Gertie in the dance halls.

Martha's greatest pleasure was her gardens. She enlarged the greenhouse. She grew luscious summer vegetables made possible by the twenty hours of daylight that lit the northern summers. Her flower garden was a showplace, with hundreds of daffodils, tulips, irises, jonquils and lilies of the valley.

On August 4, 1914, Martha and George were watching a movie in Dawson when a telegram was handed to George: "England is in a state of war with Germany." He immediately stepped to the stage of the theatre and read the message aloud. Twenty scarlet-coated Mounties seated together then rose to their feet and began to sing "God Save the King" (Canada's national anthem at the time). "The effect was electrical," Martha wrote. "With one move the audience was on its feet, and never in the world, I dare say, was our national anthem sung with greater fervour or more depth of feeling than in that moving picture house in that little town on the rim of the Arctic."

As the next two years passed and the war in Europe deepened, Martha prepared herself for what she knew would come. She took first-aid courses and threw herself into war work with the Red Cross and the Imperial (later the International) Order of the Daughters of the Empire (IODE).

In the spring of 1916, she wrote in her diary, "George has just come in and told me he has to enlist—that he cannot stand it any longer.... why should I hesitate or try to keep him back? Thousands, yes, millions, already have suffered the horrors of this terrible war for over a year." Donald (who had gone south to attend university) and Warren had already enlisted in the United States.

By October George had resigned as commissioner and organized two hundred and seventy-five men into the Yukon Infantry Company. One of the first to join was Lyman, now seventeen. They went to Victoria for training, and Martha went, too.

Martha had plans to go even farther. She was determined to accompany the company to England, but she knew that getting permission to travel with the troop ship would be enormously difficult. First she went to Ottawa and pulled every string she could, without suc-

Martha and George surrounded by officers on board the *SS Canada* on their way to England in 1917. Martha was the only woman among the 3,500 servicemen.

cess. Then she went all the way to Halifax where she persuaded—some say bullied—General Bigger, who was in charge of the army's transportation, to let her have her way. "But, Mrs. Black," he said, "you wouldn't want to be the only woman on board a ship with two thousand men, would you?" "General Bigger," she retorted. "I walked over the Chilkoot Pass with thousands of men and not one wanted to elope with me." General Bigger gave in.

In London, Martha offered her services to the Red Cross. Her typing courses of so many years earlier were put to good use, and she spent each day working in their offices. Soon George and Lyman were sent to the front lines in Europe.

Martha's task was to administer the Yukon Comfort Fund—money sent from home to supply things such as warm socks and special treats for the Yukon soldiers.

She moved into a small apartment in London and made it a home for Yukoners on leave. Now in her late forties, she became a substitute mother to them all, visiting them in the hospital when they were wounded and pooling their rations to cook special meals when they were on leave.

As a constant booster for the Yukon, Martha also began to give illustrated talks describing its beauties. Before the war was over, she had given almost four hundred lectures throughout England. She was a witty and feisty speaker. Once, when she had not been introduced with the courtesy given the male speakers, she began by saying, "My Lord Chairman, my lords, ladies, and gentlemen, if this be the way you usually treat women who are invited to address you I do not wonder suffragettes go around with axes over here."

Both George and Lyman fought bravely. George was wounded and spent several months in English hospitals. Lyman was awarded the Military Cross. Warren and Donald both returned home safely.

The war ended on November 11, 1918. George, Martha and her three sons had all survived.

13

MARTHA BLACK, M.P.

W**HEN** Martha and George returned to Canada, they found that their old way of life had disappeared. The three boys were on their own (Lyman had decided to stay in the army). The population of Dawson was now scarcely more than one thousand people. George's position had been merged with another, and Government House had been closed.

Now, in the middle of their lives, they would have to start over. Back to Vancouver they went, where George once more took up his law practice. For the next couple of years Martha enjoyed herself gardening in the gentle climate of British Columbia and speaking to women's groups about her experiences. But George's practice was not very successful, and money was a constant problem.

In 1921 George was invited to run in the federal election for the Yukon Conservatives. After a strenuous campaign, he was elected as part of the small opposition, and he and Martha moved to Ottawa. They began spending the winters there, while Parliament was in session, and the summers back in Dawson. The trip between the two was 6,500 kilometres (4,000 miles). They travelled by

Heading out from Dawson in the Model T, to make the long trip to Ottawa. "We sped along in the bracing air," wrote Martha. "It was a clear, cold aurora night, with gorgeous prism-coloured northern lights flaming and dancing across the heavens." Before reaching Ottawa, they would travel by horse-drawn stage, coastal steamer and two separate trains.

horse-drawn stage and train from Dawson to the coast, by boat to Vancouver, then across the country by train.

George was a popular politician and continued to be re-elected. He played an important part in changing the laws related to mining regulations in the Yukon and, although he had once been an ardent hunter, he now became a conservationist. The huge spring migration shoots had been banned through a U.S.-Canada convention. "It seemed a shame to kill the birds—they were so beautiful," George was quoted as saying in 1930, "and I think that almost all sportsmen who have had a surfeit of good hunting reach a stage where camera-hunting appeals as strongly as the gun."

Martha had always been interested in conservation, and now she was very careful about which wildflowers she picked, always leaving those that were in short supply. George and Martha published a book called *Yukon Wild Flowers* with a text by Martha and photographs by George. "Together we have tramped the Yukon trails and paddled the Yukon streams," Martha wrote, "he with his camera slung over his shoulder. Over the years he has taken literally hundreds of pictures of Yukon wild life, animal and floral." The little publication formed the beginning of the recorded history of plant life in that part of the country.

During these years, Martha was eager to try her hand

Martha and Lyman canoeing.

at journalism. Although she had problems getting her work accepted, she did have a few articles published, mainly about the Yukon and about her experiences on the Chilkoot Trail.

Martha's family was spread out now. Her father had died during the war after losing his fortune on poor investments, and her mother was in poor health. Although Lyman continued to visit, Warren and Donald were busy with their own lives in the United States.

Martha and George's financial problems continued. The salary of an M.P. was not very large at that time. With all the travelling between Ottawa, Vancouver and Dawson, it was difficult to have a real home life. Martha once joked that her tombstone should read, "She has only moved again."

After the 1930 election victory, George was made the Speaker of the House of Commons. Martha enjoyed being "Wife of the Speaker." She loved the pomp and ceremony, and the entertaining. But the country was now at the beginning of a deep depression that would affect everyone for most of the decade.

As the next few years went by, George began to behave more and more strangely. He developed a reputation for eccentric behaviour as Speaker and, finally, in 1935, he had a complete nervous breakdown and was hospitalized in London, Ontario. Martha's financial problems were worse than ever. She was about to turn seventy and feared that this might be the last time she would be able to return to her beloved Yukon.

It was a bleak period in their lives, but Martha's adventures were not yet over. She was about to begin a new career once more.

When it became known in the Yukon that George would be unable to run for election again, there was great consternation about whom the party should nominate as a candidate. For many years the Conservative Party had won on the strength of George Black's personal reputation. The local joke was that there were two parties in the Yukon—the Liberals and the Blacks! Now, they began to say, why not ask the other Black to run?

This was very much the way Martha saw the invitation she received to run in George's place. "I am not ambitious in the least," she wrote, "but I will not let Bennett [leader of the Conservative Party] nor the Party down."

Martha later described the 1935 campaign vividly:

My campaign was different from any other in Canada. There were only 1,805 registered voters in a territory of over 200,000 square miles—the largest constituency in Canada in area and the smallest in population. There were no radio broadcasting stations. I held only seven public meetings. To reach voters I had to travel by plane, row and motor boat, steamer, two-horse team, and the old reliable "shank's mare." I once walked several miles to visit three voters, one of whom had declared himself "agin" me. But it was worth it, for those voters had to walk eight miles to vote. (I am told I got all three votes.) Another time my car got mired in two feet of mud, and I had to tramp miles to get assistance. In my river travels sometimes the engine of my small boat would go dead in mid-stream. This meant forced landings on uninhabited shores, where frequently we came upon herds of caribou, flocks of ptarmigan, or the odd bear cub, to which I could at least rehearse my campaign speeches without being heckled.

When the election came, the Conservatives lost seats all across the country, but Martha, running as an Independent-Conservative (not aligned with the party itself) won in the Yukon—by 134 votes. She would be a member of the Opposition in the House of Commons—the second woman in history to be elected to that body. (The first was Agnes Macphail, who had been elected in 1921, the first election in which women were allowed to vote.) A few weeks later Martha celebrated her seventieth birthday.

The following year Martha carried out her duties in the House, but she never felt that she really belonged there—she was just holding the seat for George, who was now out of the hospital but remained behind in Vancouver. It was also the most painful year of her life. Lyman, the closest of her sons, was killed in a car accident. Within the next few months her oldest son, Warren, and George, her brother, had both died.

Martha carried on in spite of her sorrow. A journalist, Elizabeth Bailey Price, had come to Ottawa to interview her and was so taken by the stories of Martha's eventful life that she stayed to help her write her autobiography. *My Seventy Years* was published in 1938 and was received enthusiastically. In 1976 it was updated with the help of a Yukon writer, Flo Whyard, and published as *My Ninety Years*.

When the next election was called in 1940, George was back on his feet and it was he, once more, who ran in the Yukon and was returned to Ottawa.

Martha was perfectly happy to go back to being a wife. She was still full of energy, still fond of beautiful clothes, still delighted in entertaining, and was now a grandmother to Warren's three children. She continued to give lectures over the next decade. When she spoke to the Women's Press Club in 1947, at eighty-three years of age, one journalist wrote that she "stole the show," speaking with "all the zest and joie de vivre of a young girl," a woman "too rare for fiction and too good to be true."

Martha Black was made a Fellow of the Royal Geographical Society in 1917, and received the Order of the British Empire "for service in the development of social and cultural life, especially in the Yukon Territory" in 1949. She died on November 1, 1957, at the age of ninety-one. Tributes to "the first lady of the Yukon" flooded in. On her death, Prime Minister John Diefenbaker said, "By her courage and daring in pioneer times, by her faithfulness to the Parliament of Canada as a member of the House of Commons, and by her energy, wit and sincerity, she made a contribution to this country rarely equaled by any other woman."

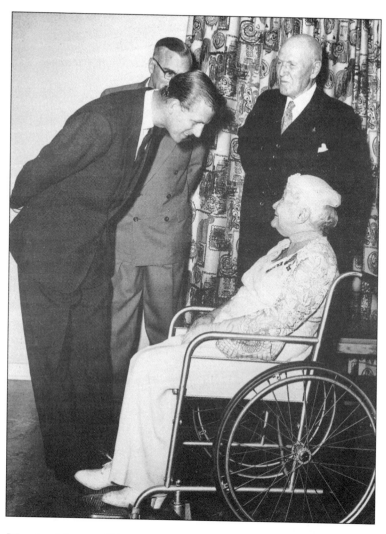

Martha Munger Black, as she often signed her name, and her husband, George, talking with Prince Philip in Whitehorse in 1954, three years before her death. A fractured hip forced her into a wheelchair during the last few years of her life.

GLOSSARY

antibiotics – substances such as penicillin and streptomycin, used to treat infectious diseases

argonauts – originally the men in Greek legend who went with Jason to find the Golden Fleece; later used to describe those who joined in the gold rushes

bootleggers – smugglers

botany – the study of plants

buckram – a coarse cotton fabric

bustle – a frame or pad worn over the buttocks by women in the nineteenth century, to accentuate their figures

cheechako – a Native word used to describe a newcomer to the Yukon or Alaska

convent – a community of Catholic nuns, or the school for girls run by them

dysentery – a painful, feverish disease caused by bacteria in food or water

elocution – the art of speaking in public, with appropriate voice and gestures

euchre – a card game played by two or four players

feisty – brave, daring

gingham – cotton fabric woven in solids, stripes or checks

glacier – ice formed from compacted snow; it slides slowly down mountains, either melting at a lower level or entering the water as an iceberg

hardtack – hard biscuits of flour and water, usually used in the army or navy

hearse – a large car used to carry a coffin for burial

herbarium – a scientifically organized collection of dried plants

infantile paralysis – poliomyelitis (polio), a serious disease once common in children

lithography – a printing process in which the image is drawn on a flat stone or plate

lodestar – a star, usually the North Star, used to guide travellers

malaria – a disease accompanied by chills and fever, transmitted by a bite from an infected mosquito

midge – a small fly

missionary – someone sent to a foreign country to teach religion or to do educational or charitable work

Norfolk jacket – a loose-fitting, belted man's jacket with box pleats in the front and back

placer gold – particles of gold found in sand or gravel, and large enough to be separated by water

prostitute – someone who sells his or her body for sexual purposes

ptarmigan – a northern bird of the grouse family, white in the winter

ragtag-bobtail – an outdated, insulting, slang expression, referring to social outcasts

seminary – a school for higher education, often a private school for girls

shank's mare – travelling by foot (usually shanks' mare)

speakeasy – an illegal bar

suffragettes – an early word for women who worked to get the vote for all women, from *suffrage*, meaning the right to vote

tin-horn gambler – a flashy, pretentious gambler

trousseau – the special clothing put together by a bride

Turkish bath – a sauna or steam bath

typhoid – a severe, infectious fever

SUGGESTIONS FOR FURTHER READING

Some other books that tell the story of the Yukon gold rush and Martha Black:

My Seventy Years by Mrs. George Black, as told to Elizabeth Bailey Price. Toronto: Nelson, 1938. *My Ninety Years* by Martha Louise Black, edited and updated by Flo Whyard. Anchorage, Alaska: Northwest Publishing, 1976. The most detailed and personal accounts of Martha Black's life are found in these two versions of her autobiography. They are written in a lively and accessible way and, although both are now out of print, they can often be found in libraries.

Klondike: The Last Great Gold Rush 1896–1899 by Pierre Berton. Toronto: McClelland & Stewart, reprinted 1993. Pierre Berton was born in Dawson and has written a number of books about the Klondike gold rush. This is the most complete account of the period.

I Married the Klondike by Laura Beatrice Berton. Toronto: McClelland & Stewart, reprinted 1993. This is a charming, personal account by Pierre Berton's mother of her years in Dawson from 1907 to 1932. It is full of details about the people and day-to-day life in the Yukon.

Klondike Women: True Tales of the 1897–1898 Gold Rush by Melanie J. Mayer. Athens, Ohio: Swallow, 1989. *Women of the Klondike* by Frances Backhouse. Vancouver: Whitecap, 1995. Two books that tell the stories of the brave women who made it to Dawson during the gold rush.

One Man's Gold Rush: A Klondike Album by Murray Morgan, photographs by E.A. Hegg. Seattle: University of Washington, 1967. A large-format book of photographs taken by the most famous photographer of the Yukon gold rush.

The True Story of the Klondike Gold Rush: A Yukon Colouring Book by Flo Whyard, drawings by Dereen Hildebrand, and *The True Story of Martha Louise: A Yukon Colouring Book* by Flo Whyard, drawings by Cathy Deer. Whitehorse: Beringian Books, 1987. Two colouring books, one including a brief story of the gold rush, the other some of the incidents in Martha Black's life, written by the journalist who worked with Martha on her second autobiography.

ACKNOWLEDGEMENTS

The best accounts of Martha Black's life lie in her two published auto-biographies, and in her diaries and letters. All of the direct quotes in this book come from her own writing.

Flo Whyard, Martha's friend and biographer, was kind enough to give me her advice and to read the manuscript. I am grateful for her help. Her own full-scale biography of Martha Black should be available soon.

Staff members at the Dawson City Museum and Historical Society, the Yukon Archives, the National Archives of Canada, the Baldwin Room of the Metropolitan Toronto Reference Library, the Glenbow Archives, the Chicago Historical Society and the Museum of the City of New York were valuable in helping to locate the prints included in this book. The Belleville Public Library, as always, was the source of much of my research.

I particularly wish to thank Janet Lunn, for reading and discussing the manuscript; my editor, Shelley Tanaka, for her wise and gentle advice; and Patsy Aldana, for suggesting I take on the project.

A grant from the Ontario Arts Council helped me to complete the writing, and I am grateful for their assistance.

PICTURE CREDITS

Front cover: Photo by E.A. Hegg, National Archives of Canada/C-5142.

Frontispiece: Yukon Archives, Munger Family Collection, 78/112.

12: The Great Fire at Chicago, October 8th, 1871. Currier & Ives. Museum of the City of New York 56.300.84 The Harry T. Peters Collection.

22: Victorian Fashions and Costumes from Harper's Bazar: 1867-1898, edited by Stella Blum. Toronto: General, 1974.

25: Chicago Historical Society, Broadside, ICHi-06185: Goes Lithographing Company, 1893.

31: Victorian Fashions and Costumes from Harper's Bazar: 1867-1898, edited by Stella Blum. Toronto: General, 1974.

38: Photo by E.A. Hegg, Special Collections Division, University of Washington Libraries, Negative # 58.

41: Photo by H.J. Woodside, National Archives of Canada/PA-16156.

45: Photo by E.A. Hegg, National Archives of Canada/C-5142.

46: Photo by E.A. Hegg, National Archives of Canada/C-1277.

48. Photo by LaRoche, National Archives of Canada/C-28649.

50: Photo by E.A. Hegg, Special Collections Division, University of Washington Libraries, Negative # 3059.

51: Photo by E.A. Hegg, National Archives of Canada/C-28619.

57: Glenbow Archives, Calgary, Alberta, NA-1786-8.

60 top: Yukon Archives, Imprint Collection, B921 Bla.

60 bottom: Yukon Archives, Martha L. Black Collection, 82/218, H-14.

63: Yukon Archives, National Museum of Canada Collection, 742.

69: Photo by E.A. Hegg. Charles W. Lindemann Collection, PH984R.47-2, Dawson City Museum and Historical Society.

74: Metropolitan Toronto Reference Library, S167 Anne Merrill Papers.

78 detail: Yukon Archives, Gillis Collection, 4531.

80: Yukon Archives, Martha L. Black Collection, 3254.

82: National Archives of Canada, C-6118.

85: Metropolitan Toronto Reference Library, S167 Anne Merrill Papers.

86: Photo by George Black, Metropolitan Toronto Reference Library, S167 Anne Merrill Papers.

91: Yukon Archives, MacBride Museum Collection, 3598.